Dr. Nightingale's Workbook for Mental Health During a Pandemic

By Lois V. Nightingale, Ph.D.

Nightingale Rose Publications

16960 E. Bastanchury Rd., Suite J.

Yorba Linda, CA 92886

Published by

Nightingale Rose Publications
16960 E. Bastanchury Rd., Suite J.
Yorba Linda, CA 92886

Library of Congress Catalog Card Number: 1-9086519181

ISBN: 978-1-889755-17-5

Disclaimer
This book is intended to provide information regarding the subject matter covered. It is not designed to take the place of professional counseling. If a person is having a particularly difficult time handling issues they are facing, they should seek professional help. If a person is experiencing signs of depression, severe anxiety reactions, or other psychological disturbances, it is important they receive professional help. Licensed therapists in your area can be found by contacting your insurance company or online under "Psychologists," or "Counselors."

Acknowledgments:
I would like to thank my biggest ally, Mike, who encouraged the creation of this book to support people during this difficult time and fed me delightful meals made with abundant love, throughout the process. Also, appreciation to Baz Here and Bambi Here for their editing and enthusiastic support.

CONTENTS

INTRODUCTION

I have been addressing mental health concerns and providing therapy for people struggling with emotional issues since the early 1980s. In no time over the last four decades have I ever seen a greater challenge for so many people than during the fallout from this COVID-19 pandemic.

People who have gracefully maneuvered divorces, business closures, life-threatening illnesses, and addictions, are now overwhelmed by the current situation. No one was prepared for this global pandemic. It is science fiction come to life. At times the ever-changing mandates and advice on how to stay safe confuse and anger people more often than they provide reassurance.

Millions of people are affected by the fear, depression, grief, confusion, overwhelm, relationship issues, child concerns, financial panic, job loss or insecurity, as well as isolation and the unpredictability of life during this global health crisis are.

In this workbook, I have kept the explanations brief (and provided books for further reading if you would like more information). I have focused on actual interventions available to people who may be struggling. This book is meant to give simple straightforward skills that individuals or groups can use.

This workbook is not meant to replace professional therapy but may be used as a tool in a therapeutic setting or group. If you are experiencing severe symptoms such as suicidality, consequences of addictions, panic attacks or severe anxiety, or outbursts of rage and anger, it is important to reach out and accept professional help. If you are suffering, it is okay to ask for assistance during these unprecedented times. Hotline phone numbers are provided in the appendix.

I invite you to read this book with a pen in your hand to make notes as you go. This workbook is set up for daily journaling and keeping track of your mental health journey. There are 30 journaling pages at the end of this workbook. Copy at least one page before you write on it, make copies, and create a three-ring binder for more journaling pages.

On these journaling pages you will have the opportunity to keep track of many topics every day, every week, or just once, as you choose. Some coping skills may already be part of your normal regime, in which case you may document and give yourself credit for what you are already doing, or you may find new skills to support your mental health that you would like to also incorporate into your life. It is not necessary to keep track of every category. You may find it most beneficial to pick the two or three categories that you feel will make the most impact on your happiness, and consistently complete those entries in your journaling pages.

You may find that some coping skills might work for someone else but not for you. Your friend may find gardening relaxing and calming. You may not like digging in the dirt and find that it just increases your stress. You might decide to read a good book in a comfortable chair instead. You are not like anyone else. Be honest with yourself. Check in with yourself and find what works best for you.

Working with a therapist or a support group as you work on your personal growth can be helpful. You may find support in having a close friend or relative who will do these exercises with you. Invest in your mental health, you are worth it!

Most of all, be kind to yourself. If you put this workbook down for days, weeks, even months and then come back to it, give yourself credit for the work you have done and are committed to doing in the future. Self-awareness is the first step to protecting your mental health and feeling more peaceful.

Checking in with yourself by completing these workbook pages may keep you more centered during challenging times or it may even spark life-changing internal conversations that over time may assist in profound differences in your life. Compliment yourself for even reading to this point in the workbook. You are worth the dedication you make to yourself, your mental health and your peace of mind.

CHAPTER ONE: EXHAUSTION FROM AVOIDING DANGER

Every day the news reports more deaths, more illness, more contradictory advice, more danger, and more unrest. Humans become exhausted when forced to be hypervigilant and wary of danger for long periods of time. Some of us might find entertainment in visiting a haunted house or amusement park adventure, but when danger is real and requires us to change our lifestyles for our safety and that of others, it is no longer amusing.

We are surrounded right now by so many issues that call for our attention. Whether we perceive every threat as dangerous as someone else sees it, we still know that others are scared. We may find ourselves walking on eggshells and obsessing about everything we say or do.

This hypervigilance takes a toll. It can take a while to adapt to a new habit or standard. While that new automatic habit is being formed, it may take extra focus and effort for a while. This increased awareness and self-reflection does take energy. Be compassionate with yourself. Activities or interactions that used to be on autopilot may now take concentration, rehearsal or even difficult conversations.

Remind yourself that you are safe. Remind yourself that you can take actions to create safety. Remind yourself that you are responsible for your own actions and your own piece of mind.

Limit your news exposure. Disconnect from social media for a while. Force yourself to read or listen to positive or humorous content. Force yourself to comment on what is going right or what you are grateful for. If you know someone who is worried, let them know they are not alone. Don't try to talk other people out of their feelings, just be a calm presence for them.

I am tired of _____

I want an end to _____

I can limit my exposure to other people's fear by_____

When I start obsessing about fear I can _____

CHAPTER TWO: CONFINEMENT

Most of us have never experienced the sense of confinement and restriction that has accompanied this COVID-19 global pandemic. Enjoying diverse settings in our day or at least on weekends, is what humans are used to doing. With so many of the activities we used to rely on for entertainment and socializing now closed or significantly restricted, many people are suffering from "cabin fever."

Although there are many introverts who are comfortable isolating at home, they may still be uncomfortable with the mask requirements or the obstacles they experience to obtain items they want or go places they wish to visit.

To add to this stress, it may seem like the recommendations and safety requirements change every day. Just as we adapt to one set of restrictions and restraints, they change and we must readjust our expectations and often our plans. Some people tolerate these moving targets better than others.

Many people of all ages are finding themselves stuck at home with household members they previously had found ways to avoid or limit their contact with. They could escape or find reprieve by going to school, to work, to visit relatives, participate in sports or other away-from-home activities. Fewer things are harder on mental health than feeling trapped with someone who is emotionally, verbally or physically dangerous.

Humans are social creatures. Isolation, imprisonment, "getting the silent treatment," time-outs, expulsions, and exiles are all punishments meant to create emotional and psychological pain. For many people the safety of social distancing can feel like an undeserved punishment.

The psychological fallout from lack of human contact can build slowly and can become unbearable over time. It is essential to be honest with yourself about your own personal need for social interaction. Just because someone close to you desires less or significantly more socializing, do not let that shame you into ignoring your own truth.

If you are uncomfortable going to a group event, however small, don't go. If you need more time on the phone or in video calls, don't let loved ones talk you out of the contact you need for your personality. (Make sure you are getting adequate sleep as well.) Interacting may take planning such as setting up an agreed upon time for a video call or planning an outdoor activity with a friend. All this extra preparation may be annoying, but it is the price to maintain some level of social interaction that is psychologically and emotionally needed.

If you are waiting for someone to call or email you, initiate contact. This is not time to keep score. People are overwhelmed, confused, struggling to find the energy for necessary daily tasks. Many people are struggling with oppressive depression or disabling anxiety. Reach out first. Reach out often. Reach out without keeping track of who initiates the contact. Reach out because it is what is needed right now. If you can think of someone who "gets" you, a person who lifts you up and energizes you, send them a message, let them know you are thinking of them. You may not know until years later that they needed to hear from you as much as you needed to interact with them.

- I am more of an   EXTROVERT   INTROVERT (circle one).

(*Quiet: The Power of Introverts in a World That Can't Stop Talking,* by Cain, is a wonderful book that explains how introverts can regain their energy that may be drained by interacting with others.)

- Two people who I have found energizing in the past _____
_____

- The way I prefer to interact with friends and family _____
_____

(In person, phone, email, messaging, video, one on one, in gatherings, etc.)

- I am committed to reach out and contact_____ this week.
- I am committed to sending _____ to _____ this week.

If you are in a challenging situation at home let someone outside your home know what is happening. (National Domestic Violence Hotline 1-800-799-7233 or 1-800-787-3224 for TTY, or if you're unable to speak safely, you can log onto thehotline.org or text LOVEIS to 22522. ChildHelp National Child Abuse Hotline 800-422-4453 www.childhelphotline.org or call 911)

CHAPTER THREE: RADICAL ACCEPTANCE

Radical acceptance is "completely and totally accepting something from the depths of your soul, with your heart and your mind," according to Marsha Linehan (*Building a Life Worth Living: A Memoir* by Linehan).

While using coping skills (provided in upcoming chapters) can help you cope with uncomfortable emotions and provide some distraction, there are some emotions and situations that require acknowledgment and acceptance. They need to be addressed directly, head-on.

Some examples are feeling helpless in the face of a loved one's addiction, sadness after the death of a friend or family member, or even the loneliness and devastation of a global pandemic. Acknowledging your pain in the face of life-changing situations can help you honor your loss, respect yourself and the real-life challenges you are facing.

It is useful and helpful to practice coping skills to relieve some of your distress, but these activities and strategies should help you get back to center, they shouldn't be about constantly distracting yourself from reality. If a coping skill is used exclusively to numb your feelings, it could be an addiction. Sometimes total acceptance takes time. Our minds must work to accept realities we don't know exactly how to handle. Be kind to yourself.

Accepting life on life's terms is one of the most difficult tasks people struggle with. We humans are hardwired to find answers, figure out solutions, build better mouse traps, find ways to get things done quicker and more effectively. Innovation and problem-solving are part of what makes us human.

But there are things over which we have no control. This is a frustrating truth, but a truth none-the-less. While hope can be a wonderful emotion, misplaced hope can create exasperation and resentment. Being honest with ourselves is sometimes the hardest task of all.

Figuring out what is actually true is an important aspect of determining what you can and cannot control. Some ways you can fact check news and claims you may come across are:

- Politifact.com (Most recognized with many awards including winner of 2009 Pulitzer Prize. Has "Truth-O-Meter," which ranks claims as True, Mostly True, False, and the notorious, Pants on Fire.)

- FactCheck.org (Started in 2003 as a project of Annenberg Public Policy Center of the University or Pennsylvania. Focuses on claims made in the political arena.)

- Flackchecker.org (A part of FactCheck.org that focuses on false claims in advertising in science and healthcare.)

- OpenSecrets.org (A part of Center for Responsible Politics that tracks campaign money and money spent on lobbying)

- Snopes.com (The granddaddy of fact checking. Started in order to address urban legends.)

- Sunlight Foundation (Uses public data to bring greater transparency to reporting.)

- Media Bias Fact/Check (A bias meter of fact checkers. It focuses on biases of reporting and fact checkers.)

- Poynter.com MediaWise (tools for figuring out what is true and worth your time.)

- *Washington Post's* Fact Checker (A blog that evaluates claims by politicians and political organizations and sometimes the media as well.)

- Hoax-Slayer.com (A site dedicated to debunking internet rumors.)

- News Literary Project (Dedicated to fact checking but is also a source to learn how to obtain resources and find a credible source in journalism.)

Even when we acknowledge that there are things we can't control; it can still be a challenge to differentiate between what we can and cannot influence. In these dynamic times of a global pandemic and civil unrest the things we can have an impact on may even change day to day.

Peace of mind is contingent on being able to accept what we have no power over and placing our focus on what we can control. Not always an easy job. But every ounce of energy we waste on obsessing about things we cannot do anything about, is an ounce of energy we could have spent on addressing something we could change. Think of positive actions you are able to take and situations where you can make a difference.

The serenity prayer, "Grant me the serenity to accept the things I cannot change, the courage to change the things I can, and the wisdom to know the difference," is a very powerful reminder of this internal process.

Three things I wish I could control but can't: _____

_____

_____

Three things I do have control over: _____

_____

_____

One tool I can use to differentiate between what I can and cannot control is:_____

_____

Three ways I can fact check if an event, statistic, or opinion is actually true before I decide if I have any control over it:

_____

_____

_____

CHAPTER FOUR: BOREDOM

We have become accustomed to the greatest variety of entertainment humans have ever known. The music choices, story-telling menus and sight-seeing options are beyond the wildest imaginations of even the royal classes of our ancestors.

We have acclimated to having unlimited choices for amusements and distractions. Being bored was more of a choice or a symptom of depression rather than arising out of the restrictions one one's movements, or limitations on sporting events, entertainment venues and impediments to vacation options.

So many of our plans have had to be cancelled or delayed until some unknown date. Family celebrations have been canceled or modified. Weddings, baby showers, birthdays, graduations, holiday traditions, retirement parties, celebrations of life, all the gatherings with food, laughter and tears that humans count on for the marking of time and acknowledging important rites of passage, are on hold or significantly different than they were.

Along with the frustration and emotional and financial loss, comes boredom. We have grown accustomed to breaking up the tedium of life with gatherings where we enthusiastically cheer on teams or live musicians or take pictures to remember important milestones in life. The loss of these important aspects of life can create boredom and even depression.

There are those who are finding ways to participate in modified versions of these events. Sports with few spectators, drive-by birthday celebrations and video parties are a few.

It is important to participate in the activities you used to do, but in modified ways. Write a list of group activities you used to enjoy. What is a modified version of each activity that may be available now?

- One group activity I used to enjoy:_____
- A modified version that may be available to me: _____

CHAPTER FIVE: COMPASSION FATIGUE

Some may be tempted to think only essential workers are vulnerable to compassion fatigue, but that is not true. Anyone who is a kind and caring person can, under the right circumstances, can suffer from compassion fatigue.

Compassion fatigue is characterized by physical and emotional exhaustion from investing too much in caregiving activities. This leads to a diminished ability to empathize or relate to others with compassion. Apathy, even anger may replace a previous kind and caring attitude. Compassion fatigue is a negative consequence of contributing care and worry about others for too long. It is sometimes viewed as secondary post-traumatic stress disorder because a caregiver may be negatively affected by listening to and caring for someone who is in or has survived a trauma.

Many people are stuck at home caring for dependent family members at levels much higher than before the pandemic. People who had breaks by going to the office to work or sending their kids to school, camp, or sports activities or had older members of the family in care facilities may be overwhelmed at the new levels of energy required to keep households in order and meet everyone's needs. Even just watching the news and feeling compassion for the escalating numbers of families affected by illness and death, can take a toll on empathetic people.

The answer to compassion fatigue is self-care and remembering you are not the only solution to the problem, even if it seems that way.

Find ways to say, "no." Look for ways to delegate and lower your standards.

If you find yourself apathetic or just not caring anymore, ask yourself what you can do to rejuvenate yourself and recharge your own emotional batteries.

- I sometimes think I am the only one who can:_____

- I can tell when I'm emotionally exhausted when I: _____

_____

- An activity I find rejuvenating is (Chapter 12 lists ideas):_____

CHAPTER SIX: PAST TRIUMPHS, OBSTACLES ALREADY SURVIVED

When life-altering challenges show up it can be difficult to believe we have the skills to cope. A great way to challenge this fear is to recall a past difficulty that you have been through.

You already have a hero inside you that has survived tough times. The best part of you remembers the strategies and resources that have helped you through previous challenges. A strong part of you has already developed skills that have seen you through previous disasters.

The past situation you bring to mind may have been initiated by others, circumstances, genetics or even yourself. What is important to remember is that you made it through. You used resources (friends, books, classes, tenacity, will-power, mentors, podcasts, videos, hope, faith, groups, biographies, personal strengths, etc.) to get through. Even if you felt pain, experienced loss, wished others had stepped up more, or felt you could have done better, you still made it through. You are still that resilient person.

- Write about a difficult time you have survived in the past. Outline why it was overwhelming and challenging.

_____

_____

_____

_____

_____

- List all the resources you used to get though that situation.

_____

_____

_____

_____

_____

- Think of something you can give yourself credit for and compliment yourself.

CHAPTER SEVEN: GRATITUDE JOURNALING

It can be challenging to think of things you are grateful for during a time when so much uncertainty and loss are globally pervasive. Training your mind to scan for what is "right," "safe," and "good," takes practice.

The research on gratitude is overwhelmingly positive. Just putting your attention on the things you appreciate in your life can create changes in how your feel, how you view the world, what you expect to happen in the future and how you perceive other people. (More information can be found in the books, *Authentic Happiness* and *Learned Optimism* by Martin Seligman.)

Each day write down 10 things you are grateful for. These can be the same or different every day. Just placing your attention on the things that are going right, the things that you wouldn't change, and the things you feel lucky for, all force your mind to practice new ways of processing information.

The things you write do not need to be grand or profound. They can be everyday mundane items such as having a place to live, being able to see, having food to eat. You may also break each of these down into subcategories such as, a room in your home that you enjoy, why you enjoy your home, or what you enjoy doing in your home, what visual beauty you enjoy, or what foods you particularly enjoy or how you attain that food. Everything you are grateful for can be broken down into subcategories of more things you can also be appreciative of.

I am grateful for:

1._____

2._____

3._____

4._____

5._____

6._____

7._____

8._____

9._____

10._____

Bonus items of appreciation:

11._____

12._____

13._____

14._____

15._____

16._____

17._____

18._____

19._____

20._____

CHAPTER EIGHT: AFFIRMATIONS

When life feels out of control our mind tends to repeat fearful and pessimistic statements over and over. An affirmation is a positive statement that is said in the present tense as if it were already true. The intention is to retrain the mind away from negative and pessimistic thinking to more positive assumptions. An affirmation may not seem true at first, but with repetition it will help change automatic negative thoughts or pessimistic mental habits into ones that add to more serenity and joy.

An affirmation needs to include the *presence* of something, never the absence. Such as, "I am safe and calm," not, "I am not in danger" or "I am not stressed." Leave out words like, "not," "isn't," "can't," "won't," "don't," "shouldn't," etc.

An affirmation must be stated *in the present*, not in the future or in the past. Such as, "Today I am safe and calm," not, "I used to be safe and calm," or "I will someday be safe and calm."

An affirmation must be *about yourself*, not others. Such as, "I am safe and calm," not, "My kids believe they are safe and calm."

One affirmation is a great place to start. If you wish to create more or change them each day, that is fine, but not necessary. Write out one affirmation and then say it silently or out loud throughout your day. (You can read more about affirmations in the book, *21 Days to Master Affirmations* by Louise Hay.)

My affirmation:

_____

_____

Tally how many times each day you repeated your affirmation.

Day 1. _____

Day 2. _____

Day 3. _____

Day 4. _____

Day 5. _____

Day 6. _____

Day 7. _____

CHAPTER NINE: BREATHING EXERCISES

In difficult times people tend to focus on the past, comparing it positively, longing for it, idealizing it or ruminating about regrets. They also tend to anticipate the future, with dread, negative expectation, hopelessness or catastrophizing. The present moment does not hold anxiety or regret. The moment happens right now. The more we can live in the present the less anxiety and depression are problems.

Focusing on your breathing is a shortcut to rejoining the present moment. You cannot breathe enough today to not have to breathe tomorrow. Breathing in and of itself is a present moment activity.

A simple to focus on the breath is to say silently to yourself, "Re----lax." Breathe in through your nose while you say, "Re…." and out through your mouth as you say, "…lax." Breathe 15 times repeating, "Re….lax," with each breath.

A more complicated breathing exercise includes sensory awareness as well. Sensory awareness is what you see, hear, smell, taste and feel. Along with breathing, what you perceive through your senses only happens in the moment. What you remember seeing is a memory, what you imagine tasting in the future is a fantasy. The actual experience of the senses only happens in the moment.

Place your tongue on the roof of your mouth just behind your front teeth. If you find your mind wondering during this exercise, press on the roof of your mouth to remind yourself to be in the present.

Breathe in through your nose to the count of four. Completely fill your lungs and expand your rib cage.

Hold your breath for the count of seven.

Exhale through your mouth (tongue still on the roof of your mouth) for the count of eight. There should be a slight sound as you exhale. This auditory sensory awareness is an additional signal to remind you to stay present in the moment. Do this for twenty breaths at least twice a day.

There are many breathing exercises available on YouTube.com, SoundCloud.com, and ones that come with personal fitness devices. Find one you like and practice it twice a day. If you practice a breathing exercise regularly it will be much more effective at helping you get back in the moment when anxiety or discouragement tug at you.

A breathing exercise I want to practice is: _____

I will practice this exercise _____ times a day.

CHAPTER TEN: ACTS OF SERVICE

When we feel scared, depressed, or anxious, it can be difficult to think about others, sometimes in fear, we even blame others for our situation. Taking actions that reach out and help others may take the last bit of energy you can find. But turning your thoughts from focusing on how bad you feel to how you can enrich the lives of others, even slightly, is a powerful tool.

This can be as simple as sending a thank you card or email, letting someone know you are thinking of them, "liking" something they posted, delivering a case of water to a nonprofit organization, generously letting someone merge in front of you in traffic, or smiling at someone who looks stressed.

Things I did today to enhance someone else's experience without expecting anything in return:

1._____

2._____

3._____   .

4._____

CHAPTER ELEVEN: SELF-CARE

Self-care is often difficult when people feel overwhelmed or exhausted. They may even be worried that they will appear selfish. But the old saying, "Put your own oxygen mask on first, and then help those around you," is truer now than ever before.

Starting with activities you currently do or things you have done in the past, may be easier than starting a whole new menu of self-care activities. Relaxing forms of exercise, artistic endeavors, activities around curiosity and tranquility are all good. (Listening to music, taking a walk, taking to a friend, taking a long bath with music and candles, reading a book, playing an instrument, making your favorite food, giving yourself a pedicure or facial, organizing photos, taking a nap, slowing down, complimenting yourself, keeping to a schedule, getting medical care, etc.) Learning a new skill, learning to say "no" or "later" even taking out time to be quiet and alone are also forms of self-care.

Things I used to do to nurture and care for myself:

1. _____

2. _____

3. _____

4. _____

5. _____

Things I did today for self-care and self-nurturance (it is okay to repeat activities if you did them more than once):

1. _____

2. _____

3. _____

4. _____

5. _____

CHAPTER TWELVE: NEW HABITS/COPING SKILLS

When you find yourself weighed down with uncomfortable feelings such as loneliness, anxiety, worry, sadness or anger, coping skills can help you deal with these emotions in healthy ways. Healthy coping skills can help soothe you, provide a temporary distraction, provide positive outlets and help you tolerate the emotional discomfort.

Coping skills and new positive habits may seem similar to self-care skills, and so they are. New skills may take some time and energy to learn, then they too can become self-care abilities. I encourage you to stretch your imagination and explore coping skills you haven't used before as well.

I have a close friend who dresses up more when she feels down. She helps herself feel better and looks great when she feels off her game. The fancier she is decked out, the worse she probably felt when she was getting dressed. It is her coping skill.

Maybe you have never drawn with chalk on your sidewalk or back patio. Maybe you have never listened to a different type of music or read a different genre of books. Maybe someone close to you has a hobby or coping skill you would like to learn. Maybe you have never slept in or gotten up early. Maybe the things others do to cope with feelings (sing in their car, listen to comedians, dress up, cook an extravagant meal, etc.) are things you have criticized and never seriously considered.

Read through this list of examples of coping skills.

Place a checkmark (√) beside the coping skills you are currently using.

Put a plus sign (+) beside the ones you would like to add to your coping skills.

Put a question mark (?) beside the items you would like to learn more about (look up online, watch YouTube videos or listen to podcasts on, etc.).

___ Exercise (jump rope, jog, go kayaking, work out)

___ Jog in place to music

___ Do yoga

___ Use a relaxation or meditation app

___ Sit and relax all your muscles

___ Stand up and stretch your muscles

___ Write out your day's schedule

___ Write a to-do list

___ Write (letters, in a journal, fiction, nonfiction, a screen play, etc.)

___ Draw doodles or scribbles

___ Write your memoir

___ Write poetry or flash fiction

___ Color in a coloring book

___ Draw a picture

___ Paint with brushes or your fingers

___ Spend time with other people (by video, phone or one at a time in person)

___ Watch a TV series

___ Watch a movie (alone or online with friends, Houseparty, Gaze, MyCircleTV, Netflix Party, TwoSeven, Scener or Rabbit are a few ways).

___ Do a word search, crossword puzzle or Sudoku

___ Research your family genealogy

___ Go on a virtual tour of a museum or a place in nature

___ Rollerblade or skateboard

___ Practice a musical instrument

___ Learn to read music

___ Go snowboarding or sledding

___ Go swimming

___ Go backpacking or hiking

___ Learn outdoor baking and cooking (you can always start with S'mores)

___ Hum a song from your childhood

___ Take a quick walk outdoors to clear your head

___ Garden, mow your lawn, trim a tree, plant flowers or vegetables

___ Take up bee keeping

___ Can fruit or vegetables, make jams and jellies

___ Work in the garage on a project

___ Fix sprinklers

___ Repair something you have been waiting to fix

___ Complete something you have been putting off

___ Organize a drawer or closet

___ List 10 positive things about yourself

___ Say, "I got this"

___ Paint a room or a wall

___ Paint your nails or those of your child

___ Watch a YouTube video on makeup, then do your own

___ Deep condition your hair

___ Give yourself a facial

___ Sing along to your playlist

___ Take a long shower

___ Take a bubble bath with music

___ Look for images in clouds

___ Rest in a hammock

___ Feed ducks, birds or squirrels

___ Go outside and look at the phase of the moon

___ Drive where you can see shooting stars

___Put a puzzle together

___ Play a card game or board game

___ Hang up a punching bag to punch

___ Allow yourself cry

___ Pray

___ Take a nap

___ Spend time with your pets

___ Pet an animal

___ Watch animal videos

___ Browse your favorite shopping sites

___ Clean something, methodically

___ Knit, crochet, sew or quilt

___ Do macramé

___ Do needlepoint or embroidery

___ Watch cooking YouTube videos for ideas

___ Create or build something

___ Restore old furniture

___ Watch a funny video

___ Go to a shooting range

___ Go to an archery range

___ Hit a bucket of balls at a golf course

___ Read a good book

___ Read those magazines waiting to be read

___ Listen to music

___ Create a new playlist

___ Smell aromatherapy

___ Meditate or do guided imagery (Follow along with one on SoundCloud or YouTube)

___ Close your eyes and relax

___ Visualize your favorite place with lots of details

___ Bake cookies

___ Try a new recipe

___ Shoot hoops, kick a ball, hit a birdie (shuttlecock)

___ Write a thank you note to someone

___ Tell someone you are thankful for them

___ Dance to music you love

___ Go for a long drive

___ Get a new pet

___ Explore a new hobby

___ Sell something online

___ Make a gratitude list

___ Perform a random act of kindness for someone

___ Read inspirational material

___ Contact a helpline or therapist

___ Reach out to a close family member or friend

___ Go for a bike ride

___ Memorize a monologue, verse, poem or song

___ Watch nature (birds, fish, wildlife, changing seasons, etc.)

___ Plan a video meeting

___ Go through old photos, make a photobook online to send someone

___ Build and fly a kite

___ Research going back to school or a career change. (The book, *What Color Is Your Parachute? 2020: A Practical Manual for Job-Hunters and Career-Changers* by Bolles, can give you ideas.)

___ Play a video or computer game, invite someone to play with you

___ Clean up trash at a park or beach (take before and after pictures)

___ Watch sports

___ Relax near water

___ Take a walk out in nature

___ Call, message or text someone

___ Rearrange furniture or pictures

___ Wear soft, comfortable clothes

___ Wrap up in a blanket

____ Make a healthy snack

____ Drink some tea

____ Sit in the sun (with sunscreen)

____ Laugh by yourself or with friends or family

____ Research a topic of interest

____ Play darts

____ Make a gift for someone

____ Schedule a video conference with a friend for lunch or dinner

____ Send an encouraging email

____ Create a video to inspire others

____ Make a video recording the stories of older family members

____ Ask for a break

____ Do a craft project

____ Take pictures (learn photography skills as well)

____ Scan old photos

____ Scan important documents

____ Take slow, deep, full breaths

____ Think of something funny

____ Take a time out to re-center

____ Count to ten slowly

____ Say kind things to yourself

____ Think of something happy

____ Practice good sleep hygiene

____ Think of a goal you would like to attain

____ Play with a stress ball

____ Look back through pictures you've taken

____ Forward a picture to make someone smile

____ Write a list your positive qualities

____ Do something kind

____ Do an activity you love

____ Play with clay

____ Make slime

____ Write something bothering you, rip the paper into pieces

____ Write an encouraging note

____ Ask yourself, "What's the upside of this?"

____ Blow bubbles outdoors

____ Chew gum

____ Blow and pop bubblegum bubbles

____ Blog about your life

____ Read a joke book

____ Laugh out loud

____ Drink cold water

____ Draw stick people cartoons

____ Count meditatively to 100

____ Make a list for the future

____ Read inspirational quotes

____ Compliment yourself

____ Visualize a stop sign

____ Smile in the mirror

____ Smile with your eyes at others

____ Stare at an object, notice every detail

____ Notice 5 things you can see, hear, and feel right now

____ Plan a fun trip

____ Identify and rate your emotions from 1 to 10

___ Share your feelings with someone

___ Write down your thoughts

___ Identify a positive thought

___ Ask yourself, "What do I want right now?"

___Make a list of choices

What are new habits you would like to incorporate into your life?

_____

_____

_____

How can you increase the chances of doing these (set alarms on your phone, make a commitment to someone else, practice, put them in your schedule, pay ahead such as for a class, personal trainer, physical therapy, etc.)?

_____

_____

CHAPTER THIRTEEN: CREATING, COOKING, GARDENING

This chapter is another aspect of self-care and skill-building.

When so many previously fulfilling activities have been shut down or are unavailable due to the pandemic, it is important to participate in endeavors that do bring a sense of accomplishment. Part of being a human is to crave making a difference. Many of the activities that gave people a sense of mattering in the world, have become unavailable. It can be difficult to develop new hobbies. There is a learning curve and you have to be willing to be a newbie before you develop proficiency. Most people find the fulfillment worth the investment.

Starting with component parts that you then transform into something new, can help create a sense of control or at least the feeling of having an impact on something.

Woodworking projects, cooking, baking, sculping, painting, knitting, quilting, gardening, landscaping, interior design, construction, husbandry all provide the experience of creating change.

- I would like to learn: _____
- The first step to explore this is: _____

CHAPTER FOURTEEN: ACKNOWLEDGING EMOTIONS

Emotions are sometimes uncomfortable and sometimes wonderful. The two most important things to remember about emotions are: 1.) They always change. They are dynamic like the weather; they are always morphing into something different. 2.) No one ever has just one emotion, ambivalence (feeling more than one way) is the natural state for humans. Sometimes these feelings may be conflicting and even seem opposite from each other. This is normal.

Emotions are sometimes strong and sometimes barely noticeable. That is why rating their intensity on a scale of 1 to 10 can also help to identify more specifically how you feel.

After you identify the emotions you are experiencing, write a coping skill or self-care item next to each uncomfortable feeling.

Many people find it hard to talk about how they feel or address painful emotions because they do not have a ready vocabulary for these internal states.

The following is a list of feeling words to choose from:

Comfortable feelings: Open, Calm, Centered, Content, Fulfilled, Patient, Pleased, Peaceful, Relaxed, Serene Trusting, Joyful, Amazed, In Awe, Blissful, Delighted, Eager, Ecstatic, Energized, Engaged, Enthusiastic, Excited, Free, Happy, Inspired, Invigorated, Lively, Passionate, Playful, Radiant, Refreshed, Rejuvenated, Renewed, Satisfied, Thrilled, Vibrant, Courageous, Powerful, Adventurous, Brave, Capable, Confident, Daring, Determined, Grounded, Proud, Strong, Worthy, Valiant, Connected, Loving, Accepting, Affectionate, Caring, Compassion, Empathetic, Fulfilled, Safe, Warm, Curious, Fascinated, Interested, Intrigued, Involved, Grateful, Appreciative, Blessed, Fortunate, Humbled, Lucky, Moved, Thankful, Hopeful, Encouraged, Expectant, Optimistic, Trusting, Tender, Reflective, Self-loving, Serene, Vulnerable.

Uncomfortable Feelings: Angry, Annoyed, Agitated, Aggravated, Bitter, Contemptuous, Cynical, Disdainful, Disgruntled, Disturbed, Edgy, Exasperated, Frustrated, Furious, Grouchy, Hostile, Impatient, Irritated, Irate, Moody, On Edge, Outraged, Pissed, Resentful, Upset, Vindictive, Sad, Anguished, Depressed, Despondent, Disappointed, Discouraged, Forlorn, Gloomy, Grief-stricken, Heartbroken, Hopeless, Lonely, Longing, Melancholy, Sorrowful, Tearful, Unhappy, Upset, Weary, Yearning, Disconnected, Numb, Aloof, Bored, Confused, Distant, Empty, Indifferent, Isolated, Lethargic, Listless, Removed, Resistant, Shut Down, Uneasy, Withdrawn, Embarrassed, Ashamed, Humiliated, Inhibited, Mortified, Self-conscious, Useless, Weak, Worthless, Fearful, Afraid, Anxious, Apprehensive, Frightened, Hesitant, Nervous, Panic, Paralyzed, Scared, Terrified, Worried, Fragile, Helpless, Sensitive, Touched Guilty, Regretful, Remorseful, Sorry, Powerless, Impotent, Incapable, Resigned, Trapped, Victimized, Stressed, Tense, Panicked, Burned out,

Cranky, Depleted, Exhausted, Frazzled, Overwhelmed, Rattled, Rejected, Restless, Shaken, Tight, Weary, Worn Out, Unsettled, Doubtful, Concerned, Dissatisfied, Grouchy, Hesitant, Perplexed, Questioning, Reluctant, Shocked, Skeptical, Suspicious, Ungrounded, Unsure.

Today I felt: _____ (1 to10): _____

Coping Skill I can use: _____

Today I felt: _____ (1 to10): _____

Coping Skill I can use: _____

Today I felt: _____ (1 to10): _____

Coping Skill I can use: _____

Today I felt: _____ (1 to10): _____

Coping Skill I can use: _____

Today I felt: _____ (1 to10): _____

Coping Skill I can use: _____

Today I felt: _____ (1 to10): _____

Coping Skill I can use: _____

CHAPTER FIFTEEN: REFRAMING. WHAT'S PERFECT ABOUT THIS?

Mental Reframing is thinking about a situation in a different way. For instance, if you now work from home you may say, "This is a disaster I am never going to be able to get anything done with the kids interrupting me all day!"

A mental reframing statement might look like, "This is challenging, but I am privileged to be able to make memories with my kids during this historical time."

Since most of us have been socialized to look for danger and the downside of situations, this may seem like a challenging skill to learn. But with some practice, you can learn how to reframe, and it eventually can even become your default way of evaluating new situations and uncomfortable emotions.

One of the prompts I personally use to think up alternative narratives is, "*What part of this perfect?*"

Perfect may seem like a stretch, but I like to challenge myself to come up with an aspect of the difficult situation that is actually perfect, meaning I wouldn't change that part of it at all.

For instance, when I'm stuck in traffic and feel agitated and annoyed, I ask myself, "How is this perfect?" I can then remind myself this gives me time to engage in activities I often don't have time for, such as listening to music, practicing relaxation breathing or listening to audiobooks. "This is perfect, I can finish that audiobook I haven't had time to get to," is a conclusion that follows my question to myself, "*What part of this is perfect?*"

Think of a situation you find yourself complaining about or that makes you upset. Notice that there is another facet of the situation that you may have minimized but noticing it creates more relaxed feelings. Compliment yourself for finding another aspect of the situation.

A situation I find upsetting: _____

The part of it that is okay (or maybe even perfect):_____

_____

Something I am upset about is: _____

One part of this that is good is: _____

One thing I complain about is:_____

One facet of this that I enjoy is: _____

One condition that infuriates me is: _____

The part of this that gives me hope is:_____

CHAPTER SIXTEEN: SLEEP HYGIENE

One of the most overlooked contributors to mental health issues is sleep deprivation and other sleep issues. With so many concerns and losses during this pandemic many people are lying awake fretting and obsessing. Getting adequate sleep is essential for serenity and emotional balance. If you are experiencing sleep issues, make it a priority to address these. Do not just assume they will resolve themselves. Ask your primary care physician, or other health professional about your options. Ask about supplements or over the counter alternatives as well. (A book you may find helpful is, *The Promise of Sleep: A Pioneer in Sleep Medicine Explores the Vital Connection Between Health, Happiness and a Good Night's sleep*, by William Dement.)

Sleep deprivation may cause:

1. Decreased performance and alertness
2. Memory and cognition impairment
3. Health problems: heart disease, high blood pressure, stroke, diabetes
4. Depression and suicidal thoughts
5. Lowered immune system
6. Low sex drive
7. Aging skin
8. Weight gain
9. Impaired judgement
10. Increased risk of death
11. Osteoporosis
12. Accidents
13. Increased cancer risk
14. Stress and irritability
15. Increased anxiety
16. Poor problem solving
17. Slower reaction times
18. Intensified emotions
19. Impaired neuron production

Important Things to Implement to Address Sleep Issues:

1. Have a set bedtime with a relaxing routine, make it the same every night.
2. No caffeine after noon (none is even better).
3. Daily exercise (outdoors in the sun if you can) for at least 30 minutes.
4. Create a dark and quiet room with no TV or computer on while sleeping.
5. Turn off all electronic screens 1 hour before sleep.
6. No alcohol or refined sugar before sleep.

7. Set an alarm for 8-9 hours of sleep.

8. Take medications/supplements at the same time every night (set phone alarm if you need to.)

9. Write down "to do" items that may keep you awake worrying about them.

10. Have a cool temperature in your bedroom.

11. Charge all kids' electronics in the parents' room.

12. Check kids' histories on computer/phone/text—no digital interaction after bedtime.

13. Meditate or use relaxation techniques if you can't go right to sleep until you drift off.

14. Talk with your medical provider about medications or supplements like melatonin, chamomile tea or Valerian Root.

My sleep record (total hours slept in 24 hours, time you went to sleep and woke up, factors that may have influenced these results, etc.):

Day 1: _____

Day 2: _____

Day 3: _____

Day 4: _____

Day 5: _____

Day 6: _____

Day 7: _____

CHAPTER SEVENTEEN: COMMITMENTS

Very little will bring us down faster or create more anxiety than our own perception that we have not kept a commitment. Keeping our word seems to be an import aspect of mental health for humans. (A short book that addresses the value of keeping your word is *The Four Agreements*, by Don Miguel Ruiz.)

When people feel overwhelmed, exhausted, depressed or are grieving, keeping commitments may go by the wayside. It is important to be kind and patient with yourself if you are struggling right now.

If you are normally a high-integrity person who shows up and keeps your word, remember that those aspects of yourself are still a part of you. Right now, it may be important to cut yourself slack, make fewer commitments and be willing to change your mind and reevaluate situations one by one as they show up.

Complimenting yourself on the commitments you are currently keeping, however small and insignificant they may seem, is an act of self-compassion. Did you get up on time, shower, return one phone call, go for that walk, or pay that bill? Give yourself credit. What you focus on gets stronger. Don't beat yourself up. Acknowledge the small tasks that represent the way you want to be.

Today I followed through on: _____

Today I followed through on: _____

Today I followed through on: _____

CHAPTER EIGHTEEN: LIMIT DRAINING ACTIVITIES

Activities that you used to have time and energy for, may now seem daunting and more than you can handle. It is okay to say "no," or, "maybe later." It is okay to reprioritize what is important and what you actually have the energy and focus to accomplish.

(The book, *Codependent No More* by Beattie, has more information about over-extending yourself, as does, *Meditations for Women Who Do Too Much* or *Meditations For People Who (May) Worry Too Much* by Schaef.)

Make a list of draining activities, i.e., watching the news, listening to your in-laws, waiting for a significant other, things you have been talked into but don't really want to do, taking on another pet, a family Zoom meeting, etc.. You might decide to continue to participate in some of these activities but do so consciously. Know how you are going to feel.

Don't agree to activities and commitments that will build resentment. Feeling resentful comes from saying "yes" when you really need to say "no." Choose carefully what you watch, listen to, participate in, contribute to, wait for, and agree to.

Draining activities I am staying aware of and may choose to limit:

- _____

- _____

- _____

CHAPTER NINETEEN: DISENGAGING FROM ZERO-SUM ARGUMENTS

A zero-sum game is when one competitor wins a point the other competitor must lose a point. So, the sum of the score is always zero. The goal of the game/conversation is not only to win, but to demean and make the other person wrong in order to win.

One indication that you may be participating in a zero-sum game, is that you feel you are being "sold" a perspective, bombarded with lots of evidence and substantiating facts. If you find yourself defensive and explaining your perspective over and over, you may have agreed to participate in a zero-sum game.

Allowing whoever you are arguing with to perceive you inaccurately, "wrong" or differently than you see yourself, is a good way to detach from the argument. If you notice that you are becoming defensive, disengage without further debate and end the argument.

People often get entangled in zero-sum arguments because they fear, "*this will be the last argument; I have to get my point across now.*" If you are in a long-term relationship or interacting with a family member, try to remember that this is unlikely to be the very last time this issue will discussed. Put the back and forth dispute on hold. Remember there will be another time to come back to whatever the issue is.

Abusive relationships are based on defensiveness and arguing for the right to want what one wants and feel how one feels. If "no" is not an acceptable answer or walking away to cool off is met with taunts to reengage, you may be in an abusive relationship. Learning how to not react, resisting the urge to try and change the other person's mind about you, and taking time for yourself to cool off even in the face of sarcastic jabs, are essential to maintain your own serenity.

(If you think you may be in an emotionally or verbally abusive relationship a good book to read is *The Verbally Abusive Relationship* by Patricia Evans.)

When I hear, "Sure just walk away see you don't care." I will _____

_____

When I am tempted to repeatedly explain my side of an argument I will _____

_____

When I need to disengage from an argument I will _____
_____

Even when a situation seems unfair, I will _____

CHAPTER TWENTY: FINANCIAL RESPONSIBILITY

During uncertain times financial concerns are often present. When so many industries are on hold, changing substantially, or closing all together, owners, employees, customers and vendors are all affected. Whether job loss or change has affected you personally, these changes may have affected someone close to you. How money is spent or saved may change dramatically during challenging times. Many couples have never had authentic, transparent financial conversations. One or both partners may be scared or feel overly responsible when there are no open conversations about finances.

It may be tempting to ignore financial stress and follow the urge to bury your head in the sand. But staying aware of your finances, even if you must go in debt or borrow money, is important for your overall mental health.

Often fears and "what ifs" swirl around in a mind obsessing about infinite dreadful possibilities. The real numbers, what is spent and what is coming in, are finite, no matter how grim, they have limits.

Keeping track of your finances will keep you in the best position possible to handle deficits or hard decisions. Denial can lead to crisis where you may no longer have choices of your own. Staying aware of the specifics of your financial situation can also provide unexpected opportunities as well as fewer surprises.

(A great book about staying on top of your finances is, *How to Get Out of Debt, Stay Out of Debt and Live Prosperously* by Mundis. Suzie Orman also has many helpful books and podcasts.)

- Write down each of your accounts (checking, savings, investment, credit cards, lines of credit, etc.).

- Write the balances next to each account.

- Write down everything you spend every day.

- Write down income as it comes in, not before.

- Look at your list every day.

- If you are in a partnership, share these with each other weekly or monthly.

The way I will keep track of my finances is (in a ledger, in QuickBooks/Quicken, on my laptop, with Excel on a Cloud, etc._____

I will share my finances with _____

CHAPTER TWENTY-ONE: ANGER MANAGEMENT

Expressing anger at others may feel good temporarily, but it is unhealthy and not productive. Back in the early days of my training as a psychologist the theory of catharsis was popular. The theory encouraged people to express their anger in order to, "get it out." Now we know better. Any expression or repetition of anger increases, not decreases, the chances of experiencing more anger.

Neuropathways fire in the brain each time we act and these neuropathways develop more and more connections, making it more probable that a specific neuropathway will fire again in the future under a similar circumstance. Every time a frustrated person loses their temper and expresses their anger in an inappropriate way, they are upping the chances that it will happen again.

On the other hand, every time a frustrated person slows down and choses a coping skill to deal with their anger, they lower the chances of acting out and exploding in the future.

Outbursts of anger can be dismaying to loved ones, coworkers and even the person who exploded in front of others. Anger is an emotion that is not dangerous in itself, but actions and words that are expressions of this feeling may be dangerous. Anger is the emotion that protects us when we feel threatened, it is a secondary emotion to fear.

When important elements of life are unpredictable, people may experience fear and anxiety. When fear becomes unbearable or is a difficult emotion for a person to manage, anger shows up for protection.

Another, often overlooked, aspect of anger is that it is an essential phase of the grieving process. The five stages of grief are denial, bargaining, anger, sadness and acceptance. When grief is complicated and the person suffering gets stuck while processing their grief, anger is often the stage where they get stuck.

Reading about grief, participating in an online grief support group or talking with others who have suffered losses can help move through the difficult process of grief. (*The Grief Recovery Handbook, The Action Program for Moving Beyond Death, Divorce, and Other Losses including Health, Career, and Faith* by James and Friedman is a great resource.)

Anger is also a part of the defense mechanism of projection. Projection is when we notice, even condemn, a negative aspect of someone else as a way to ignore and not think about that same aspect in our own personalities. Projection is an unconscious process, so it can be difficult to observe in ourselves. Journaling or talking with a therapist about your own projections can help make these judgmental and angry assessments more conscious. What we are aware of we can then address.

Many people have been harmed by others who acted out in anger and consequently are more sensitive to displays of anger in those around them. It is important to talk about anger issues in your home. During this pandemic home needs to be as emotionally safe as possible.

Working to understand the perspective of others and building tools for empathy and compassion, can help address anger issues. Understanding that others are doing the best they can figure out, just like you are, is a powerful step to curbing outbursts of anger.

Effective anger management can transform uncomfortable emotions into better communication skills with others. Therapy, anger management classes online, or using some of the coping skills listed in Chapter 12 may help. (*The Anger Workbook* by Minirth, Frank, Carter, Les is a good resource.)

Practice giving the benefit of the doubt.

- When my child doesn't obey me, maybe: _____

- When another driver is erratic, maybe: _____

- When people don't address this pandemic the way I think they should, maybe: _____
_____

- I can forgive myself for:_____

- Something that I do that I find myself judging in others is:_____
_____

CHAPTER TWENTY-TWO: NUTRITION

So many of our rituals around the essentially human activity of sharing meals have been disrupted during this pandemic. The shared coffee, celebration dinners and going out to eat with friends and family, have all been altered.

Before changing your diet or eating patterns please check with your physician or health care provider, especially if you have underlying medical issues. I encourage people to make meals a mindful activity. Be thoughtful, eat the food you chose with intention. Nurture yourself with beautiful, healthy and lovingly prepared food.

In times of crisis or uncertainty we tend to self-nurture with "comfort food," or not eat much at all due to anxiety. Neither of these is optimal but may be temporary situations during difficult times.

Adding produce to your current diet can be a simple way to improve your eating habits. Fruits and vegetables tend to have high nutrition, lower fat, and fewer calories. The more produce you consume the less likely you are to binge on junk food.

Keep things simple. Don't take on overwhelming dietary changes that you know you cannot maintain. It's better to change things a little at a time and maintain those changes.

Refined sugar and simple carbohydrates (cookies, ice cream, pastries, white bread, soda, etc.) increase inflammation in people. Depression has been correlated with increased inflammation. Also, spikes in blood sugar with subsequent plummets after sugar is metabolized, can add to anxiety.

Eating low processed food (food that looks like it did when it was picked, pulled from the ground, butchered or caught) can help stabilize mood.

Try to eat something healthy within a half hour of waking and a small meal or snack with protein every three hours throughout your day.

Caffeine can amplify anxiety and cause sleep disturbances. Alcohol is a depressant and can also disrupt healthy sleep patterns.

Stay conscious and be kind to yourself. Small consistent changes will help the most over the long run.

- My commitment to my eating regime_____

_____

- I want to add in: _____

_____

- I want to consume less: _____

_____

CHAPTER TWENTY-THREE: EXERCISE

Next to good sleep hygiene, exercise is probably the most important nonmedical intervention you can implement for mental health.

Exercise helps burn up anxiety fight or flight chemicals. Exercise helps with good sleep. Exercise assists the brain in functioning at its best. Exercise is a stress reliever and enhances creativity.

If you have been a life-long exerciser, keep it up during difficult times. If you have never exercised, start slowly, and work up gradually. Check with your physician or health care provider before you begin any new exercise. Getting into a habit is one of the most important variables in keeping an exercise regime going. Using a digital fitness tracker may be inspiring.

Try not to go more than three days without exercising, daily exercise is a good goal.

Look up exercises that you can do even though many forms may not be available (i.e., gyms, group activities, team sports etc.). Check out YouTube and cable channels for fun follow-along exercises. Add music into your work out. Keep track of the days you find the time and energy to participate in your preferred exercise.

- Exercise_____ Time _____

- Exercise_____ Time _____

- Exercise_____ Time _____

- Exercise_____ Time _____

- Exercise_____ Time _____

- Exercise_____ Time _____

- Exercise_____ Time _____

CHAPTER TWENTY-FOUR: ADDRESSING CLUTTER

During times when so much is out of control it can be therapeutic to focus on the things you do have control over.

We have all said, "When I have the time…" Now may very well be that time. It can be difficult to address those organization projects when energy is low and anxiety high, but doing something where you can actually see an outcome, can help that feeling of helplessness.

Don't let someone else tell you what you "should" organize or clean out. Focus on the projects you care about. If that drawer in the kitchen or that corner in the garage bothers you the most, start there even if someone else thinks you should start with your closet or somewhere else.

Set aside short amounts of time to address clutter. Be very focused on what you are going to do. For instance, take 15 minutes to clean out the bottles in your shower. Take 15 minutes to organize the trunk of your car. If you have too far-reaching goals you may not start at all.

If you are cleaning out a larger area, a room, garage, patio, etc., set up five boxes. 1. Things to take to a secondhand store, 2. Things to keep, 3. Things to throw away, 4. Things to sell, 5. Things you are not sure about and will come back to later.

Compliment yourself for everything you do, even if it wasn't perfect or if you only completed a part of what you had hoped to accomplish.

(A great book to help you declutter is *Decluttering at the Speed of Life: Winning Your Never-Ending Battle with Stuff* by White.)

Three areas I would like to clean out:

- _____
- _____
- _____

The first step I need to do for each of those:

- _____
- _____
- _____

CHAPTER TWENTY-FIVE: SELF-FORGIVENESS LETTER

One of the most draining psychological problems is holding the past over one's own head. We have all made mistakes. We all have regrets. If we could turn back time with what we know now, we would all have made some other decisions.

But the truth is, we cannot go back and change the past. There are no time machines to revisit those moments we wished we had made other choices.

The only impact we can have on regret and guilt is self-forgiveness. Forgiveness doesn't mean forgetting, it means letting yourself off the hook, releasing yourself from debt and discontinuing beating yourself up for things you cannot change now.

Self-forgiveness means knowing you did the best you could figure out to do at the time. With the options you could see, the restrictions you saw, the limitations of circumstances, you made the best choice you could see, at minimum the least bad choice you could figure out at the time.

That doesn't mean there weren't consequences, to yourself or others. It doesn't mean there weren't pieces to pick up and apologies to make. It does mean that you are human, and mistakes and miscalculations are part of the human experience.

If you are beating yourself up emotionally for mistakes you made in the past, this is a good time to do the work of self-forgiveness. Being fully present in the moment is not possible if you are living in regrets of the past. Compassion and forgiveness are the paths to serenity and living fully in the present.

- I regret: _____

_____

- It's hard to forgive myself because: _____

_____

- The first step in forgiving myself is: _____

_____

- Some of the factors that kept me from doing it differently at the time were:_____

_____

Write yourself a letter: Dear _____, I forgive you for _____. I know you did the best you could at the time. I forgive_____

_____.

CHAPTER TWENTY-SIX: LETTERS TO YOURSELF FROM FIVE YEARS IN THE FUTURE

During times of change and uncertainty major decisions can be hard to make. There are many variables that go into making life choices. Emotional, financial, your integrity, family, expectations, what you've become accustomed to, health, and pragmatics, among others, all can influence decision making.

Our minds know we can't see the future, but we can remember the past. Writing a letter to yourself from five years in the future can psychologically bypass some of the inhibitions we have to looking at what is best for ourselves.

Write two letters to yourself, one for each of the paths you are deciding between. Write one as if you chose one path. Write the next one as if you had chosen the other path.

When writing the letters to yourself from five years in the future, be creative. Add to the letter over days or weeks, writing at different times of day, with different levels of fatigue or energy. Add in as many details as you can imagine. Who are you hanging out with? How much are you making? Where are you living? Where are you going on vacation? How happy are you? What are the downsides of that choice? Who is surprised at how this has turned out? What regrets do you have? Who is most proud of you? What are you doing that contributes to others?

All these answers are made up, so be creative, see where it takes you. At least you will have more perspectives to bring into the decision-making process than you did before you wrote the letters.

Dear (Yourself)_____   Date (Five years from today) _____

You decided to (first choice)_____

And now _____

_____

_____

_____

_____

Dear (Yourself)_____   Date (Five years from today) _____

You decided to (second choice)_____

And now_____

_____

_____

_____

_____

CHAPTER TWENTY-SEVEN: GROUP ATTENDANCE

We humans are social animals. This pandemic has inhibited many social activities that nurtured our need to belong, to celebrate and receive feedback from others. Much of the physical contact that nurtures humans, hugs, handshakes, even pats on the back, are now on hold. This lack of human contact can take a toll after a while.

Some people need less social interaction and some people desire more. Even the most introverted of us, still needs human contact by way of reading other people's work, seeing them smile and laugh or watching their videos, etc.

A social community can be in-person or virtual. A supportive group can be a support group (12-step, houses of worship, NAMI, partial hospital programs, etc.) a hobby group (sports, quilting, music, collections, fan clubs, etc.) an activity group, a spiritual group, a volunteer group or an educational group or class. Participation can be as simple as just showing up to a Zoom meeting and being a good listener and supporting others, or it may mean sharing or helping with organizing and maintaining the group.

Groups can be found through internet sites such as meetup.com, your house of worship, parks and recreation for your city, AA.org, Coda.org, Naranon.org. EA.org, GA.org, SA.org, or googling a hobby or artistic outlet you already have. (Most groups now meet online and have recommended reading materials or suggested videos, ask them.)

If you are struggling with an addiction or dual diagnosis (an addiction as well as a mental illness) it is particularly important that you find group support. These illnesses are better addressed with the encouragement, mentorship, and safety of an organized group (AA, NA, MA, OA, SA, GA, EA, SMART, etc.). If you are upset by someone else's addictive behavior, you may also benefit from caring group support, mentorship, and pertinent information (Ala-non, Nar-anon, Coda, O-anon, S-anon, G-anon, etc.).

It can be intimidating to attend a group for the first time. During this pandemic most groups are meeting online, which provides a little more anonymity. The support and hope that many people find in groups can expedite your mental health journey.

3 groups I might find interesting (online or in-person):

_____

_____

_____

A group I attended/logged into this week:

_____

One thing I took away from this group meeting:

_____

One thing I shared in this group:

_____

One person I found that I have something in common with (name not necessary, description is okay)

_____

CHAPTER TWENTY-EIGHT: GOSSIP VS. SUPPORT

It is normal for humans to want to talk out their problems and concerns. During pre-pandemic life most people had a wide circle of friends and family to vent to and use as sounding boards.

Now when interactions are limited, and past supportive circles are not as available it can be challenging for people to find safe communities to vent to.

If a friend or family member in inclined to keep score, hold what you share over your head later, or use the information to make themselves look good to someone else, they are not an emotionally safe person to share your vulnerable thoughts and feelings with.

If you do have emotionally safe friends or family to share with, make sure the focus of your disclosure is about yourself (i.e., "I noticed I am having a hard time not snapping at my kids" vs. "Let me tell you what horrible things my kids did!")

Complaining about others for the purpose of enlisting pity from the listener, or to find agreement that you're being victimized, is gossip. It is easier to describe a challenging situation than it is to assess and disclose how you are reacting to it. If you are venting to avoid authentic transparent self-disclosure because that is more difficult, you are avoiding and deflecting.

Gossip and deflecting may seem innocent at the time, but there is a price one pays. If a person gossips, they will automatically believe others are gossiping about them. If a person avoids and deflects, they will conclude that other people are superficial and don't want to discuss anything deep or real either. They also tend to not feel authentically supported.

Gossip is intended to triangulate and get the listener "on their side." Gossip is currency that insecure people use to make themselves feel better and create a temporary sense that they are chosen over the person they are gossiping about. Gossip is not vulnerable. It does not require courage. It is focused on gathering the support of others against the person gossiped about.

Self-disclosing for emotional support is vastly different. Self-disclosure is self-revealing and reveals a vulnerable aspect of the self. It does not focus on others, but oneself. Self-revealing tends to be shorter and contains less evidence and specific facts. Gossip is about salacious details meant to cast someone else in a disparaging light.

During this time when most people's social circles are significantly smaller, it can be challenging to stay aware if one is gossiping or sharing vulnerable self-disclosure. A good question to ask yourself is, "Am I trying to get the listener to take my side or feel sorry for me, or am I sharing something vulnerable about myself for support?" (i.e., "He leaves his dishes all over the house!" vs. "I am really struggling with my resentment about picking up his dishes.")

Journaling and writing out your thoughts can help you differentiate these two kinds of communication. Slowing down and thinking before you speak can also help. Engaging the assistance of a professional counselor can also assist you in moving towards self-disclosure for support and away from gossiping.

When I was gossiped about I felt_____

I caught myself gossiping when_____

When I'm pitied I feel_____

When I'm supported I feel _____

I wish my friends and family knew that I _____

I would like to find the words to self-disclose about_____

I am finding the courage to share _____

CHAPTER TWENTY-NINE: SOCIAL CAUSE FATIGUE

This global pandemic is not playing out in a void. The global unrest and the upheaval within individual countries are also a part of the uncomfortable landscape right now. When there is chaos and fundamental systemic change, many previously hidden issues can sift to the surface.

Most people are naturally compassionate and care about the suffering of other humans. Of course, there are a small number of exceptions, but these are not the norm.

It can be exhausting to try and figure out what causes are most important to every person you interact with. Try to remember this is true for them as well. In an atmosphere of fear and danger, other unrelated fears may be amplified and loom larger.

There are infinite social causes and injustices that demand our attention. The more centered and calm you are with yourself, the more clarity you will have to determine which causes you have energy to participate in. If you are anxious and off balance, taking care of your own mental health is important. You will be most effective in all your endeavors if you are practicing successful self-care.

Slowing down to examining your own values is essential before you can champion for others. We are a global community and any injustice affects all humans. But obsessing about the injustices in the world, while being too exhausted, too anxious, too depressed, or too immobilized to do anything productive will not help anyone.

At times addressing injustices in the world can energize people and give them a sense of purpose. For those that act with clarity and thought-out intention, these actions can be helpful and of service. Unfortunately, when people are scared and resentful, they may act more impulsively or in ways that drain them further and may not produce the hoped-for results.

Anger is the emotion that we feel when we are unsafe. Anger is a powerful feeling, fear is not. When anger becomes a predominate emotion there is fear and anxiety that need to be attended to.

There are productive ways to express anger and revulsion, but these helpful actions can only be arrived at by contemplation and planning. If you are participating in actions that are just, that you have the energy for, and that you have thought through, then they are unlikely to be destructive.

I find myself obsessing with criticism and judgment when_____

_____

_____

I catch myself focusing on problems rather than solutions when_____

_____

I notice I slip into "bonding" by complaining about others with friends and family when_____

_____

It is in my integrity to _____

My words and actions are an accurate representation of how I feel when _____

_____

My words are my own (vs. parroting others) when I talk about _____

_____

What I wish was different is _____

What I have the energy and focus to address is _____

I practice self-compassion when _____

_____

I disengage from arguments by _____

I accept incongruent aspects of myself by _____

_____

CHAPTER THIRTY: DREAM ANALYSIS

For the purposes of this workbook I am not going to go into a lot of depth on the topic of dream analysis. But since so many clients are reporting vivid dreams during these challenging times and wanting to work with them, I am going to provide some tools to work with your dreams.

One way to work with your dreams is to remember that they are symbolic. The pictures in a dream are picked by your own unconscious. Of all the things one experiences in life day in and day out, the unconscious chooses only items that symbolize issues or topics the dreamer is working on.

The language of dreams is similar to the language of myth. (You can read more about this in *The Hero's Journey*, by Joseph Campbell.)

When the unconscious is working through issues, dreams can provide insight into those concerns.

If you have a reoccurring dream it may be worth writing it down and then doing the following evaluation on the specific elements of the dream.

Since the people, places, things, events, smells, sounds, etc. in your dreams are all symbolic, they can provide information about yourself that is otherwise more difficult to access.

Start by listing all the items in your dream. For instance, a shaggy dog, a previous boss, a sidewalk, and a leash.

Then write beside each item what you believe it was *feeling* in your dream. For instance:

Shaggy dog: lonely

Previous boss: financially scared

Sidewalk: unappreciated

Leash: disconnected

Then write beside each item what you think it *wanted* in your dream. For instance:

Shaggy dog: to get out and interact with others

Previous boss: employees to be more productive

Sidewalk: to be noticed and appreciated

Leash: to connect the dog to previous boss.

In looking at the symbols in this dream you may be able to examine where you are feeling lonely, financially scared, unappreciated and disconnected. You can take a look at what different parts of you may want right now: to get out and interact with others, have others do their share, to be noticed and appreciated and to connect.

There are many deeper levels of dreams and ways to analyze them. But writing them down to look for patterns and doing the previous exercise can give you a glimpse into your own unconscious. A qualified licensed therapist may also be able to help you evaluate your dreams and what they may be able to reveal to you.

My dream:_____

_____

_____

_____

_____

Items in my dream: _____

_____

_____

What each item wanted in my dream: _____

_____

How each item in my dream felt: _____

_____

CHAPTER THIRTY-ONE: WHAT DO YOU WANT?

Many people never slow down long enough to ask themselves what they really want. This may be a good time, even amidst the pandemic, to take advantage of some down time to examine what you really want.

Some people know what everyone around them wants. They have ideas about what they "should" want. They defend why they cannot have what they want. They are acutely aware of the things they wanted that they did not get in the past. They anticipate what others will say if they reveal what they want. They are not sure they have a right to want what they want. They have been told since they were young that it is selfish to want anything. They are told only an authority can tell them what they should want. Or, they are told they must earn the right to want things.

A want is a wish. A want is a dream. A want is a desire. A want is an internal state, an experience. You *always* have a right to your hopes and dreams. They may not come true. You may not get what you want. There are many barriers to our deepest hopes and wants, but they are still valid.

Finding words for what you really want is part of good self-esteem. Being able to write or say what you want is part of taking care of yourself and being a fully functioning adult.

This does not necessarily mean your wishes will be accommodated, that is a different conversation. But even if you cannot imagine how your wish could ever come true, you still have a right to your wish.

Speak up if a loved one discounts your wants and desires. Notice if someone who cares about you indicates that you should not want something that they wouldn't want. You are a unique person. You have a right to have wishes and desires that others might not have based on their own life experiences and temperaments.

Your wants may be tangible: a different residence, a new job or car, to travel or have a new electronic item.

Your wants may be intangible: to be spoken to with respect, to feel included, to be happy, to feel less lonely, to belong.

If you find yourself focused on what others want, notice that. If you disqualify any want that shows up for you, notice that. If you feel you don't have a right to say what you want, notice that. If you tell yourself you don't have the right to want anything that is unlikely to happen, notice that. If you are having long silent debates in your mind about what you can and can't want, also notice that.

When you were a kid you probably blew out birthday candles, or wished on a falling star, making wishes that might or might not come true. It was a gift to yourself to make a wish. It is still a gift to yourself to acknowledge what you want.

If it is not emotionally, physically, or financially safe to share what you want with those close to you, don't share with them. Find emotionally and psychologically safe environments with friends, extended family, online support groups or a therapist to share them with.

I want _____

I hope that _____

I wish that _____

My biggest dream is _____

A goal of mine is _____

CHAPTER THIRTY-TWO: ROMANCE DURING A PANDEMIC

During pre-pandemic life romance could be a challenging topic. During a global epidemic it is ever so much more complicated.

Those supportive loving relationships certainly have a safety net during shelter-in-place mandates and in isolating times. Many couples are finding the slower pace, the unhurried time together and more time to communicate are all enhancing their feelings of closeness and emotional safety.

Other couples are finding the lack of distractions, decreased time apart, heightened stress reactions and past unresolved emotions are amplifying the issues that were ignored prior to the pandemic. Hunkering down together to deal with the unprecedented climate can be extremely uncomfortable for these couples. Many therapists are offering video or in-person couple counseling sessions. If you are in one of these difficult relationships, talk about what you might explore to get back to being best friends and partners during this time. (*Nonviolent Communication* by Rosenberg and *It's a Bedroom not a Boardroom* by Nightingale are resources to improve communication.)

For those who are single and looking for love, they may find more options online and more single people willing to write and talk about authentic topics due to the world circumstances. But there may be increased barriers to meeting new people face to face.

This is a good time to self-reflect and ask yourself if you are happy with yourself, proud of your life, entertained by your thoughts and creativity. This is a good time to re-evaluate what you believe makes you lovable. During this global pandemic, many people are appraising their priorities and what they believe is important. Many of the superficial traits that people traded on are suddenly not as important when everything is up in the air and uncertainty is the norm.

In romance "like attracts like."

If you want a partner with specific traits, develop those in yourself. If you are looking for someone to complete you or fix your life, you will attract someone who is looking for someone to complete themselves or someone who they can control to give them a sense of power.

If you are enthusiastic about your work, express yourself in a sport or creativity, have productive ways of coping with uncomfortable emotions, and find satisfaction in giving back to others, you will attract someone with similar values and who won't make you responsible for their happiness.

If you are looking for a life partner, look in places where people are bettering themselves (classes, self-improvement groups, houses of worship, physical fitness venues, etc.) or bettering the world (volunteer activities, contributing to causes they care about, doing acts of service in the community.) Unhealthy places to look for partners are places where people are anesthetizing their emotions (bars, parties, alcohol tastings, etc.) Places where people participate in their addictions are good places to find an addict.

Those who are in unhealthy relationships during this pandemic are in difficult circumstances. It is a hard time to change everything about your life, but many people are finding the courage to get out.

With more proximity and fewer other social contacts for distraction, people in romantic partnerships are left with close-up views of their relationship. This may motivate couples to seek assistance for communication challenges, ways to forgive past mistakes, or long-standing disagreements about relatives, finances or parenting. If both partners are motivated for change, this can be a great time to improve the relationship.

If your relationship is negatively affected by addiction (alcohol, drugs, gambling, sexual acting out, spending, eating disorders, etc.) this may be a good time to join a support group online such as Al-aon, CoDA, S-anaon, AA, NA, GA, SA, OA, DA, etc.. Meetings are virtual and you can log in from an email address you designate for just this purpose. Reach out for support. You don't have to face addictions, or the consequences of addictions, alone.

If you are in an abusive relationship, this pandemic may be amplifying the danger. A verbally, emotionally, sexually, physically, or financially abusive relationship during these unprecedented times can become unsustainable. If you think you may be the victim of abuse let others know. You may feel most comfortable talking to someone staffing a hotline or running a support group or a therapist. But keep looking for a friend or family member you can tell. The more you talk about it the more you will see the situation clearly. Don't minimize. If you feel unsafe it is likely you are. Get support and learn that you are worth finding a way out.

I would characterize my relationship as: _____

The best part of my relationship is:_____

The most important aspect of a romantic relationship is: _____

What I am unwilling to put up with: _____

What I am willing to do to work on my relationship: _____

I am unwilling to _____ for my relationship.

I am willing to work on myself for my relationship by: _____

CHAPTER THIRTY-THREE: YOU GET MORE OF WHATEVER YOU PUT YOUR ATTENTION ON

Those who are familiar with *The Secret* by Byrne, know how important it is to pay attention to what you spend time focusing on. It is a basic tenant of the human condition that whatever we think about, we tend to get more of.

People who are always looking out for someone to take advantage of them, will most likely have more experiences where they feel taken advantage of.

People who are scanning all the time for others to criticize, will inevitably find more people to condemn.

People who look for things to be grateful for will automatically find more things in their life that are good.

People who are afraid others are out to get them will experience more and more paranoia over time.

Fred Rogers shared a bit of wisdom his mother gave him as a child. "When I was a boy and I would see scary things in the news, my mother would say to me, 'Look for the helpers. You will always find people who are helping.'" Mr. Rogers learned at a young age that what you look for you tend to find.

People who attend to those who are making a difference will tend to find more evidence that there are courageous people in the world impacting issues that need addressing.

We may not have control over all the tragic events happening right now, but each of us has control over what we put our attention on and the factors we replay over and over in our minds.

What do you want to see more of? _____

What is a small example of that? _____

What do you wish you noticed more of? _____

What is a minor sample of this that you have noticed? _____

_____

CHAPTER THIRTY-FOUR: GIVE YOURSELF CREDIT

Just as what you attend to you get more of, the actions and thoughts that you give yourself credit for will develop the fastest.

When parents teach a child to walk, they don't scold and shame every time the toddler falls down. Rather, every attempt at a step, every step that ends up in a fall, every step no matter how faltering, is praised by the parents. Parents intuitively know that what they praise and applaud will continue to be practiced and will eventually lead to success.

How we speak to ourselves is the same. If you scold and shame yourself, (i.e., "You're so dumb, look you can't do anything right.") you will have less energy, less self-confidence and less likelihood of succeeding at your task.

Encouraging yourself as you try something new is essential for success. (i.e., "I'm not proficient yet, but I'm better than I was yesterday and I'm not a quitter.")

Speaking to yourself like you would a friend or loved one is important for mental health. People cannot belittle, shame or scold themselves into feeling better or finding calm. Our minds react the same way to internal scolding as they do if someone on the outside was belittling us. Give yourself the benefit of the doubt. You are doing the best you can figure out right now. Be kind. Especially to yourself.

I notice I say unkind things to myself when:_____

Instead I would like to say: _____

It's hard for me not to get mad at myself when: _____

Next time I want to say: _____

I have perfectionistic standards for myself when it comes to: _____

I will cut myself slack next time by saying: _____

CHAPTER THIRTY-FIVE: 30 DAYS OF DAILY CHARTING

Keep your daily charting pages in a safe place so you feel comfortable being as honest as possible.

Make a copy of at least one of the following pages before you fill it in so you can continue charting after you have finished the 30 pages provided.

Date:_____

Notes:_____

I am proud that I _____

10 items I am grateful for.

_____   _____

_____   _____

_____   _____

_____   _____

_____   _____

I said an affirmation _____ times today.

I did a breathing exercise _____ times today.

Something I did for someone else without expecting anything in return _____

_____

Self-care/coping skills I used today:_____

Today I felt: _____ (1 to10): _____

Today I felt: _____ (1 to10): _____

Today I felt: _____ (1 to10): _____

I slept _____ hours in the last 24: _____

Today I kept my word by: _____

I said "No" to: _____

I resisted defending myself when _____

I wrote down everything I spent today. Yes_____   No_____

I ate _____ servings of produce. I ate _____ times today. I ate _____ servings of protein. I ate ___ servings of junk food.

I exercised _____ minutes today doing _____.

I attend/logged into a group today. Yes_____ No___

I demonstrated respect for what I want today by_____

Date:_____

Notes:_____

I am proud that I _____

10 items I am grateful for.

_____   _____

_____   _____

_____   _____

_____   _____

_____   _____

I said an affirmation _____ times today.

I did a breathing exercise _____ times today.

Something I did for someone else without expecting anything in return _____
_____

Self-care/coping skills I used today:_____

Today I felt: _____ (1 to10): _____

Today I felt: _____ (1 to10): _____

Today I felt: _____ (1 to10): _____

I slept _____ hours in the last 24: _____

Today I kept my word by: _____

I said "No" to: _____

I resisted defending myself when _____

I wrote down everything I spent today. Yes_____   No_____

I ate _____ servings of produce. I ate _____ times today. I ate ____ servings of protein. I ate ___ servings of junk food.

I exercised _____ minutes today doing _____.

I attend/logged into a group today. Yes_____ No____

I demonstrated respect for what I want today by_____

Date:_____

Notes:_____

I am proud that I _____

10 items I am grateful for.

_____   _____

_____   _____

_____   _____

_____   _____

_____   _____

I said an affirmation _____ times today.

I did a breathing exercise _____ times today.

Something I did for someone else without expecting anything in return _____

_____

Self-care/coping skills I used today:_____

Today I felt: _____ (1 to10): _____

Today I felt: _____ (1 to10): _____

Today I felt: _____ (1 to10): _____

I slept _____ hours in the last 24: _____

Today I kept my word by: _____

I said "No" to: _____

I resisted defending myself when _____

I wrote down everything I spent today. Yes_____   No_____

I ate _____ servings of produce. I ate _____ times today. I ate _____ servings of protein. I ate ____ servings of junk food.

I exercised _____ minutes today doing _____.

I attend/logged into a group today. Yes_____ No_____

I demonstrated respect for what I want today by_____

Date:_____

Notes:_____

I am proud that I _____

10 items I am grateful for.

_____   _____

_____   _____

_____   _____

_____   _____

_____   _____

I said an affirmation _____ times today.

I did a breathing exercise _____ times today.

Something I did for someone else without expecting anything in return _____

_____

Self-care/coping skills I used today:_____

Today I felt: _____ (1 to10): _____

Today I felt: _____ (1 to10): _____

Today I felt: _____ (1 to10): _____

I slept _____ hours in the last 24: _____

Today I kept my word by: _____

I said "No" to: _____

I resisted defending myself when _____

I wrote down everything I spent today. Yes_____   No_____

I ate _____ servings of produce. I ate _____ times today. I ate _____ servings of protein. I ate ____ servings of junk food.

I exercised _____ minutes today doing _____.

I attend/logged into a group today. Yes_____ No___

I demonstrated respect for what I want today by_____

Date:_____

Notes:_____

I am proud that I _____

10 items I am grateful for.

_____   _____

_____   _____

_____   _____

_____   _____

_____   _____

I said an affirmation _____ times today.

I did a breathing exercise _____ times today.

Something I did for someone else without expecting anything in return _____

_____

Self-care/coping skills I used today:_____

Today I felt: _____ (1 to 10): _____

Today I felt: _____ (1 to 10): _____

Today I felt: _____ (1 to 10): _____

I slept _____ hours in the last 24: _____

Today I kept my word by: _____

I said "No" to: _____

I resisted defending myself when _____

I wrote down everything I spent today. Yes_____   No_____

I ate _____ servings of produce. I ate _____ times today. I ate _____ servings of protein. I ate ____ servings of junk food.

I exercised _____ minutes today doing _____.

I attend/logged into a group today. Yes_____ No____

I demonstrated respect for what I want today by_____

Date:_____

Notes:_____

I am proud that I _____

10 items I am grateful for.

_____   _____

_____   _____

_____   _____

_____   _____

_____   _____

I said an affirmation _____ times today.

I did a breathing exercise _____ times today.

Something I did for someone else without expecting anything in return _____

_____

Self-care/coping skills I used today:_____

Today I felt: _____ (1 to10): _____

Today I felt: _____ (1 to10): _____

Today I felt: _____ (1 to10): _____

I slept _____ hours in the last 24: _____

Today I kept my word by: _____

I said "No" to: _____

I resisted defending myself when _____

I wrote down everything I spent today. Yes_____   No_____

I ate _____ servings of produce. I ate _____ times today. I ate _____ servings of protein. I ate ___ servings of junk food.

I exercised _____ minutes today doing _____.

I attend/logged into a group today. Yes_____ No___

I demonstrated respect for what I want today by_____

Date:_____

Notes:_____

I am proud that I _____

10 items I am grateful for.

_____   _____

_____   _____

_____   _____

_____   _____

_____   _____

I said an affirmation _____ times today.

I did a breathing exercise _____ times today.

Something I did for someone else without expecting anything in return _____

_____

Self-care/coping skills I used today:_____

Today I felt: _____ (1 to10): _____

Today I felt: _____ (1 to10): _____

Today I felt: _____ (1 to10): _____

I slept _____ hours in the last 24: _____

Today I kept my word by: _____

I said "No" to: _____

I resisted defending myself when _____

I wrote down everything I spent today. Yes_____   No_____

I ate _____ servings of produce. I ate _____ times today. I ate _____ servings of protein. I ate ___ servings of junk food.

I exercised _____ minutes today doing _____.

I attend/logged into a group today. Yes_____ No____

I demonstrated respect for what I want today by_____

Date:_____

Notes:_____

I am proud that I _____

10 items I am grateful for.

_____   _____

_____   _____

_____   _____

_____   _____

_____   _____

I said an affirmation _____ times today.

I did a breathing exercise _____ times today.

Something I did for someone else without expecting anything in return _____
_____

Self-care/coping skills I used today:_____

Today I felt: _____ (1 to10): _____

Today I felt: _____ (1 to10): _____

Today I felt: _____ (1 to10): _____

I slept _____ hours in the last 24: _____

Today I kept my word by: _____

I said "No" to: _____

I resisted defending myself when _____

I wrote down everything I spent today. Yes_____   No_____

I ate _____ servings of produce. I ate _____ times today. I ate _____ servings of protein. I ate ___ servings of junk food.

I exercised _____ minutes today doing _____.

I attend/logged into a group today. Yes_____ No____

I demonstrated respect for what I want today by_____

Date:_____

Notes:_____

I am proud that I _____

10 items I am grateful for.

_____   _____

_____   _____

_____   _____

_____   _____

_____   _____

I said an affirmation _____ times today.

I did a breathing exercise _____ times today.

Something I did for someone else without expecting anything in return _____
_____

Self-care/coping skills I used today:_____

Today I felt: _____ (1 to10): _____

Today I felt: _____ (1 to10): _____

Today I felt: _____ (1 to10): _____

I slept _____ hours in the last 24: _____

Today I kept my word by: _____

I said "No" to: _____

I resisted defending myself when _____

I wrote down everything I spent today. Yes_____   No_____

I ate _____ servings of produce. I ate _____ times today. I ate _____ servings of protein. I ate ____ servings of junk food.

I exercised _____ minutes today doing _____.

I attend/logged into a group today. Yes_____ No____

I demonstrated respect for what I want today by_____

Date:_____

Notes:_____

I am proud that I _____

10 items I am grateful for.

_____   _____

_____   _____

_____   _____

_____   _____

_____   _____

I said an affirmation _____ times today.

I did a breathing exercise _____ times today.

Something I did for someone else without expecting anything in return _____
_____

Self-care/coping skills I used today:_____

Today I felt: _____ (1 to10): _____

Today I felt: _____ (1 to10): _____

Today I felt: _____ (1 to10): _____

I slept _____ hours in the last 24: _____

Today I kept my word by: _____

I said "No" to: _____

I resisted defending myself when _____

I wrote down everything I spent today. Yes_____   No_____

I ate _____ servings of produce. I ate _____ times today. I ate _____ servings of protein. I ate ___ servings of junk food.

I exercised _____ minutes today doing _____.

I attend/logged into a group today. Yes_____ No___

I demonstrated respect for what I want today by_____

Date:_____

Notes:_____

I am proud that I _____

10 items I am grateful for.

_____   _____

_____   _____

_____   _____

_____   _____

_____   _____

I said an affirmation _____ times today.

I did a breathing exercise _____ times today.

Something I did for someone else without expecting anything in return _____
_____

Self-care/coping skills I used today:_____

Today I felt: _____ (1 to10): _____

Today I felt: _____ (1 to10): _____

Today I felt: _____ (1 to10): _____

I slept _____ hours in the last 24: _____

Today I kept my word by: _____

I said "No" to: _____

I resisted defending myself when _____

I wrote down everything I spent today. Yes_____   No_____

I ate _____ servings of produce. I ate _____ times today. I ate _____ servings of protein. I ate ___ servings of junk food.

I exercised _____ minutes today doing _____.

I attend/logged into a group today. Yes_____ No____

I demonstrated respect for what I want today by_____

Date:_____

Notes:_____

I am proud that I _____

10 items I am grateful for.

_____   _____

_____   _____

_____   _____

_____   _____

_____   _____

I said an affirmation _____ times today.

I did a breathing exercise _____ times today.

Something I did for someone else without expecting anything in return _____

_____

Self-care/coping skills I used today:_____

Today I felt: _____ (1 to10): _____

Today I felt: _____ (1 to10): _____

Today I felt: _____ (1 to10): _____

I slept _____ hours in the last 24: _____

Today I kept my word by: _____

I said "No" to: _____

I resisted defending myself when _____

I wrote down everything I spent today. Yes____   No____

I ate _____ servings of produce. I ate _____ times today. I ate _____ servings of protein. I ate ___ servings of junk food.

I exercised _____ minutes today doing _____.

I attend/logged into a group today. Yes____ No___

I demonstrated respect for what I want today by_____

Date:_____

Notes:_____

I am proud that I _____

10 items I am grateful for.

_____   _____

_____   _____

_____   _____

_____   _____

_____   _____

I said an affirmation _____ times today.

I did a breathing exercise _____ times today.

Something I did for someone else without expecting anything in return _____
_____

Self-care/coping skills I used today:_____

Today I felt: _____ (1 to10): _____

Today I felt: _____ (1 to10): _____

Today I felt: _____ (1 to10): _____

I slept _____ hours in the last 24: _____

Today I kept my word by: _____

I said "No" to: _____

I resisted defending myself when _____

I wrote down everything I spent today. Yes_____   No_____

I ate _____ servings of produce. I ate _____ times today. I ate _____ servings of protein. I ate ___ servings of junk food.

I exercised _____ minutes today doing _____.

I attend/logged into a group today. Yes_____ No___

I demonstrated respect for what I want today by_____

Date:_____

Notes:_____

I am proud that I _____

10 items I am grateful for.

_____   _____

_____   _____

_____   _____

_____   _____

_____   _____

I said an affirmation _____ times today.

I did a breathing exercise _____ times today.

Something I did for someone else without expecting anything in return _____
_____

Self-care/coping skills I used today:_____

Today I felt: _____ (1 to10): _____

Today I felt: _____ (1 to10): _____

Today I felt: _____ (1 to10): _____

I slept _____ hours in the last 24: _____

Today I kept my word by: _____

I said "No" to: _____

I resisted defending myself when _____

I wrote down everything I spent today. Yes_____ No_____

I ate _____ servings of produce. I ate _____ times today. I ate _____ servings of protein. I ate ___ servings of junk food.

I exercised _____ minutes today doing _____.

I attend/logged into a group today. Yes_____ No____

I demonstrated respect for what I want today by_____

Date:_____

Notes:_____

I am proud that I _____

10 items I am grateful for.

_____   _____

_____   _____

_____   _____

_____   _____

_____   _____

I said an affirmation _____ times today.

I did a breathing exercise _____ times today.

Something I did for someone else without expecting anything in return _____
_____

Self-care/coping skills I used today:_____

Today I felt: _____ (1 to10): _____

Today I felt: _____ (1 to10): _____

Today I felt: _____ (1 to10): _____

I slept _____ hours in the last 24: _____

Today I kept my word by: _____

I said "No" to: _____

I resisted defending myself when _____

I wrote down everything I spent today. Yes_____ No_____

I ate _____ servings of produce. I ate _____ times today. I ate _____ servings of protein. I ate ___ servings of junk food.

I exercised _____ minutes today doing _____.

I attend/logged into a group today. Yes_____ No___

I demonstrated respect for what I want today by_____

Date:_____

Notes:_____

I am proud that I _____

10 items I am grateful for.

_____   _____

_____   _____

_____   _____

_____   _____

_____   _____

I said an affirmation _____ times today.

I did a breathing exercise _____ times today.

Something I did for someone else without expecting anything in return _____
_____

Self-care/coping skills I used today:_____

Today I felt: _____ (1 to10): _____

Today I felt: _____ (1 to10): _____

Today I felt: _____ (1 to10): _____

I slept _____ hours in the last 24: _____

Today I kept my word by: _____

I said "No" to: _____

I resisted defending myself when _____

I wrote down everything I spent today. Yes_____ No_____

I ate _____ servings of produce. I ate _____ times today. I ate _____ servings of protein. I ate ___ servings of junk food.

I exercised _____ minutes today doing _____.

I attend/logged into a group today. Yes_____ No___

I demonstrated respect for what I want today by_____

Date:_____

Notes:_____

I am proud that I _____

10 items I am grateful for.

_____ _____

_____ _____

_____ _____

_____ _____

_____ _____

I said an affirmation _____ times today.

I did a breathing exercise _____ times today.

Something I did for someone else without expecting anything in return _____
_____

Self-care/coping skills I used today:_____

Today I felt: _____ (1 to10): _____

Today I felt: _____ (1 to10): _____

Today I felt: _____ (1 to10): _____

I slept _____ hours in the last 24: _____

Today I kept my word by: _____

I said "No" to: _____

I resisted defending myself when _____

I wrote down everything I spent today. Yes_____   No_____

I ate _____ servings of produce. I ate _____ times today. I ate _____ servings of protein. I ate ____ servings of junk food.

I exercised _____ minutes today doing _____.

I attend/logged into a group today. Yes_____ No____

I demonstrated respect for what I want today by_____

Date:_____

Notes:_____

I am proud that I _____

10 items I am grateful for.

_____   _____

_____   _____

_____   _____

_____   _____

_____   _____

I said an affirmation _____ times today.

I did a breathing exercise _____ times today.

Something I did for someone else without expecting anything in return _____
_____

Self-care/coping skills I used today:_____

Today I felt: _____ (1 to10): _____

Today I felt: _____ (1 to10): _____

Today I felt: _____ (1 to10): _____

I slept _____ hours in the last 24: _____

Today I kept my word by: _____

I said "No" to: _____

I resisted defending myself when _____

I wrote down everything I spent today. Yes_____   No_____

I ate _____ servings of produce. I ate _____ times today. I ate ____ servings of protein. I ate ___
servings of junk food.

I exercised _____ minutes today doing _____.

I attend/logged into a group today. Yes_____ No___

I demonstrated respect for what I want today by_____

Date:_____

Notes:_____

I am proud that I _____

10 items I am grateful for.

_____   _____

_____   _____

_____   _____

_____   _____

_____   _____

I said an affirmation _____ times today.

I did a breathing exercise _____ times today.

Something I did for someone else without expecting anything in return _____

_____

Self-care/coping skills I used today:_____

Today I felt: _____ (1 to10): _____

Today I felt: _____ (1 to10): _____

Today I felt: _____ (1 to10): _____

I slept _____ hours in the last 24: _____

Today I kept my word by: _____

I said "No" to: _____

I resisted defending myself when _____

I wrote down everything I spent today. Yes_____   No_____

I ate _____ servings of produce. I ate _____ times today. I ate _____ servings of protein. I ate ___ servings of junk food.

I exercised _____ minutes today doing _____.

I attend/logged into a group today. Yes_____ No___

I demonstrated respect for what I want today by_____

Date:_____

Notes:_____

I am proud that I _____

10 items I am grateful for.

_____   _____

_____   _____

_____   _____

_____   _____

_____   _____

I said an affirmation _____ times today.

I did a breathing exercise _____ times today.

Something I did for someone else without expecting anything in return _____

_____

Self-care/coping skills I used today:_____

Today I felt: _____ (1 to10): _____

Today I felt: _____ (1 to10): _____

Today I felt: _____ (1 to10): _____

I slept _____ hours in the last 24: _____

Today I kept my word by: _____

I said "No" to: _____

I resisted defending myself when _____

I wrote down everything I spent today. Yes_____   No_____

I ate _____ servings of produce. I ate _____ times today. I ate _____ servings of protein. I ate ____ servings of junk food.

I exercised _____ minutes today doing _____.

I attend/logged into a group today. Yes_____ No____

I demonstrated respect for what I want today by_____

Date:_____

Notes:_____

I am proud that I _____

10 items I am grateful for.

_____   _____

_____   _____

_____   _____

_____   _____

_____   _____

I said an affirmation _____ times today.

I did a breathing exercise _____ times today.

Something I did for someone else without expecting anything in return _____

_____

Self-care/coping skills I used today:_____

Today I felt: _____ (1 to10): _____

Today I felt: _____ (1 to10): _____

Today I felt: _____ (1 to10): _____

I slept _____ hours in the last 24: _____

Today I kept my word by: _____

I said "No" to: _____

I resisted defending myself when _____

I wrote down everything I spent today. Yes_____   No_____

I ate _____ servings of produce. I ate _____ times today. I ate _____ servings of protein. I ate ___ servings of junk food.

I exercised _____ minutes today doing _____.

I attend/logged into a group today. Yes_____ No___

I demonstrated respect for what I want today by_____

Date:_____

Notes:_____

I am proud that I _____

10 items I am grateful for.

_____   _____

_____   _____

_____   _____

_____   _____

_____   _____

I said an affirmation _____ times today.

I did a breathing exercise _____ times today.

Something I did for someone else without expecting anything in return _____
_____

Self-care/coping skills I used today:_____

Today I felt: _____ (1 to10): _____

Today I felt: _____ (1 to10): _____

Today I felt: _____ (1 to10): _____

I slept _____ hours in the last 24: _____

Today I kept my word by: _____

I said "No" to: _____

I resisted defending myself when _____

I wrote down everything I spent today. Yes_____   No_____

I ate _____ servings of produce. I ate _____ times today. I ate _____ servings of protein. I ate ___ servings of junk food.

I exercised _____ minutes today doing _____.

I attend/logged into a group today. Yes_____ No___

I demonstrated respect for what I want today by_____

Date:_____

Notes:_____

I am proud that I _____

10 items I am grateful for.

_____   _____

_____   _____

_____   _____

_____   _____

_____   _____

I said an affirmation _____ times today.

I did a breathing exercise _____ times today.

Something I did for someone else without expecting anything in return _____
_____

Self-care/coping skills I used today:_____

Today I felt: _____ (1 to10): _____

Today I felt: _____ (1 to10): _____

Today I felt: _____ (1 to10): _____

I slept _____ hours in the last 24: _____

Today I kept my word by: _____

I said "No" to: _____

I resisted defending myself when _____

I wrote down everything I spent today. Yes_____   No_____

I ate _____ servings of produce. I ate _____ times today. I ate _____ servings of protein. I ate ____ servings of junk food.

I exercised _____ minutes today doing _____.

I attend/logged into a group today. Yes_____ No____

I demonstrated respect for what I want today by_____

Date:_____

Notes:_____

I am proud that I _____

10 items I am grateful for.

_____   _____

_____   _____

_____   _____

_____   _____

_____   _____

I said an affirmation _____ times today.

I did a breathing exercise _____ times today.

Something I did for someone else without expecting anything in return _____
_____

Self-care/coping skills I used today:_____

Today I felt: _____ (1 to10): _____

Today I felt: _____ (1 to10): _____

Today I felt: _____ (1 to10): _____

I slept _____ hours in the last 24: _____

Today I kept my word by: _____

I said "No" to: _____

I resisted defending myself when _____

I wrote down everything I spent today. Yes_____   No_____

I ate _____ servings of produce. I ate _____ times today. I ate _____ servings of protein. I ate ___ servings of junk food.

I exercised _____ minutes today doing _____.

I attend/logged into a group today. Yes_____ No___

I demonstrated respect for what I want today by_____

Date:_____

Notes:_____

I am proud that I _____

10 items I am grateful for.

_____   _____

_____   _____

_____   _____

_____   _____

_____   _____

I said an affirmation _____ times today.

I did a breathing exercise _____ times today.

Something I did for someone else without expecting anything in return _____
_____

Self-care/coping skills I used today:_____

Today I felt: _____ (1 to10): _____

Today I felt: _____ (1 to10): _____

Today I felt: _____ (1 to10): _____

I slept _____ hours in the last 24: _____

Today I kept my word by: _____

I said "No" to: _____

I resisted defending myself when _____

I wrote down everything I spent today. Yes_____   No_____

I ate _____ servings of produce. I ate _____ times today. I ate _____ servings of protein. I ate ___ servings of junk food.

I exercised _____ minutes today doing _____.

I attend/logged into a group today. Yes_____ No___

I demonstrated respect for what I want today by_____

Date:_____

Notes:_____

I am proud that I _____

10 items I am grateful for.

_____   _____

_____   _____

_____   _____

_____   _____

_____   _____

I said an affirmation _____ times today.

I did a breathing exercise _____ times today.

Something I did for someone else without expecting anything in return _____
_____

Self-care/coping skills I used today:_____

Today I felt: _____ (1 to10): _____

Today I felt: _____ (1 to10): _____

Today I felt: _____ (1 to10): _____

I slept _____ hours in the last 24: _____

Today I kept my word by: _____

I said "No" to: _____

I resisted defending myself when _____

I wrote down everything I spent today. Yes_____   No_____

I ate _____ servings of produce. I ate _____ times today. I ate _____ servings of protein. I ate ____ servings of junk food.

I exercised _____ minutes today doing _____.

I attend/logged into a group today. Yes_____ No____

I demonstrated respect for what I want today by_____

Date:_____

Notes:_____

I am proud that I _____

10 items I am grateful for.

_____   _____

_____   _____

_____   _____

_____   _____

_____   _____

I said an affirmation _____ times today.

I did a breathing exercise _____ times today.

Something I did for someone else without expecting anything in return _____
_____

Self-care/coping skills I used today:_____

Today I felt: _____ (1 to10): _____

Today I felt: _____ (1 to10): _____

Today I felt: _____ (1 to10): _____

I slept _____ hours in the last 24: _____

Today I kept my word by: _____

I said "No" to: _____

I resisted defending myself when _____

I wrote down everything I spent today. Yes_____   No_____

I ate _____ servings of produce. I ate _____ times today. I ate ____ servings of protein. I ate ___ servings of junk food.

I exercised _____ minutes today doing _____.

I attend/logged into a group today. Yes_____ No___

I demonstrated respect for what I want today by_____

Date:_____

Notes:_____

I am proud that I _____

10 items I am grateful for.

_____   _____

_____   _____

_____   _____

_____   _____

_____   _____

I said an affirmation _____ times today.

I did a breathing exercise _____ times today.

Something I did for someone else without expecting anything in return _____
_____

Self-care/coping skills I used today:_____

Today I felt: _____ (1 to10): _____

Today I felt: _____ (1 to10): _____

Today I felt: _____ (1 to10): _____

I slept _____ hours in the last 24: _____

Today I kept my word by: _____

I said "No" to: _____

I resisted defending myself when _____

I wrote down everything I spent today. Yes_____   No_____

I ate _____ servings of produce. I ate _____ times today. I ate _____ servings of protein. I ate ____
servings of junk food.

I exercised _____ minutes today doing _____.

I attend/logged into a group today. Yes_____ No____

I demonstrated respect for what I want today by_____

Date:_____

Notes:_____

I am proud that I _____

10 items I am grateful for.

_____   _____

_____   _____

_____   _____

_____   _____

_____   _____

I said an affirmation _____ times today.

I did a breathing exercise _____ times today.

Something I did for someone else without expecting anything in return _____
_____

Self-care/coping skills I used today:_____

Today I felt: _____ (1 to10): _____

Today I felt: _____ (1 to10): _____

Today I felt: _____ (1 to10): _____

I slept _____ hours in the last 24: _____

Today I kept my word by: _____

I said "No" to: _____

I resisted defending myself when _____

I wrote down everything I spent today. Yes_____   No_____

I ate _____ servings of produce. I ate _____ times today. I ate _____ servings of protein. I ate ____
servings of junk food.

I exercised _____ minutes today doing _____.

I attend/logged into a group today. Yes_____ No____

I demonstrated respect for what I want today by_____

Date:_____

Notes:_____

I am proud that I _____

10 items I am grateful for.

_____   _____

_____   _____

_____   _____

_____   _____

_____   _____

I said an affirmation _____ times today.

I did a breathing exercise _____ times today.

Something I did for someone else without expecting anything in return _____

_____

Self-care/coping skills I used today:_____

Today I felt: _____ (1 to10): _____

Today I felt: _____ (1 to10): _____

Today I felt: _____ (1 to10): _____

I slept _____ hours in the last 24: _____

Today I kept my word by: _____

I said "No" to: _____

I resisted defending myself when _____

I wrote down everything I spent today. Yes_____   No_____

I ate _____ servings of produce. I ate _____ times today. I ate _____ servings of protein. I ate ____ servings of junk food.

I exercised _____ minutes today doing _____.

I attend/logged into a group today. Yes_____ No____

I demonstrated respect for what I want today by_____

APPENDIX

Hotline Contact Information:

National Suicide Prevention Lifeline Hours: Available 24 hours. Languages: English, Spanish. 1-800-273-8255

National Alliance on Mental Illness: 800-950-6264 nami.org

Alcoholics Anonymous: AA org,

SMART Recovery: smartrecovery.org

Anxiety and Depression Association of America: adaa.org

National Institute of Mental Health: https://www.nimh.nih.gov/

Find a Therapist: PsychologyToday.com or GoodTherapy.org

Made in USA - North Chelmsford, MA
1176132_9781889755175
10.07.2020 0633